**This book belongs to:**

_____

*For my dad Philip, who showed me how to use
many tools and always encouraged me.*

– Zoë


*To ML – may your curiosity always guide me.*

– Anja

First edition published in 2022 by Flying Eye Books,
an imprint of Nobrow Ltd. 27 Westgate Street, London, E8 3RL.

Text © Zoë Armstrong
Illustrations © Anja Sušanj

Expert consultant: Dr Elisa Bandini

Zoë Armstrong and Anja Sušanj have asserted their rights under the Copyright, Designs and
Patents Act, 1988, to be identified as the Author and Illustrator of this Work.

Every attempt has been made to ensure any statements written as fact have been checked to
the best of our abilities. However, we are still human, thankfully, and occasionally little mistakes
may crop up. Should you spot any errors, please email info@nobrow.net.

1 3 5 7 9 10 8 6 4 2

Published in the US by Nobrow (US) Inc.
Printed in Poland on FSC® certified paper.

ISBN: 978-1-83874-001-6
www.flyingeyebooks.com

Zoë Armstrong          Anja Sušanj

# Curious Creatures
# WORKING
# WITH TOOLS

Flying Eye Books

Earth is a busy place. Listen hard and you might hear the sounds
of a billion little tasks being tackled all around the planet.

Tasks that we tackle using tools . . .

Like brushing our teeth,

making breakfast,

or hammering in a tent peg.

People use tools in all kinds of ways. You might say it's part of what makes us human. But did you know that a small number of extraordinary animals also use tools?

In the sky, on land, and deep beneath the sea, there are creatures with brains big enough and complex enough to use objects in crafty ways. Resourceful creatures that use tools to solve problems, just like you do.

A kayak bobs gently in California's Monterey Bay. The paddlers gaze across the water as two sea otters float by on their backs.

Bash, bash, bash! One of the otters is pounding a clam against a rock on his chest to break open its shell.

*Sea otters sometimes keep a favorite stone in a baggy pouch of skin under their arms. They store food there too.*

## A Sea Otter's Toolkit

The otters are using rocks and seaweed as tools to help them solve problems and prepare a meal.

They use seaweed in other ways too. Before taking a nap in the water, these resourceful mammals will wrap themselves in long strands of kelp, so they won't drift away. Mother otters keep their pups from floating off by swaddling them in seaweed.

Zoologists think sea otters have been using tools like this for thousands or even millions of years.

*A group of resting otters,
anchored together with
kelp, is called a raft.*

The other has wound kelp around a crab so that
it can't move. She rests the snack on her chest
to eat later. Right now she's munching a mussel
she's opened with her favorite stone.

9

# What Is a Tool?

A tool is an object that is used to solve a problem. It is an object that you hold, which helps you to do a job more easily. These animals are using sticks as tools to get things done. They are solving big problems, such as finding food, and little day-to-day annoyances too . . .

## The Gorilla

In a swampy forest near Africa's great Congo River, a gorilla paddles her feet in a pool of water. The pool is wide and the water looks deep—will it be safe to cross?

The gorilla has found a tool to help. She uses a long stick as a measuring tool, which she dips into the water in front of her before wading in farther. She dips then she steps, dips then steps—steadying herself with the stick as she creeps forward.

## The Elephant

An Asian elephant in Bangladesh bats away irritating flies with a branch. Another scratches her back with a spiky stick. The elephants choose the right tool for the job. If a branch is too bushy, they break pieces off until it is just right.

## The Mandrill

A mandrill in Cameroon is busy scraping dirt from under his nails with a small twig. That's better—nice and clean.

# The Chimpanzee

A hungry chimp in Tanzania can't reach his meal, so he makes a handy tool to help. Hunched over a termite mound, he strips leaves from a twig with his mouth to make a smooth stick. Then he pokes the stick into the mound to fish out the insects. He nibbles his lively lunch like a lollipop.

## Dr. Jane Goodall

In 1960, a primatologist named Jane Goodall was working in the forests of Gombe, in East Africa. She noticed a chimp—who she called David Greybeard—using a grass stem to pull termites out of their nest. It was the first time a nonhuman animal had been recorded using a tool.

A scientist in Indonesia is exploring the ocean when he spots a curious sight. A veined octopus lolls along the seabed, hauling half a coconut shell beneath its body.

Scientists think these octopuses might once have used animal shells in this way too. When humans began chopping coconuts in half, the octopuses found an even better kind of shelter!

### JUST LIKE YOU . . .

Perhaps you have a portable shelter too. An umbrella is an object that humans carry, just in case. You can huddle beneath it whenever it begins to rain.

It's not safe out in the open, and the bulky cargo slows the octopus down. Watch out for predators!

But the creature has a plan. It finds another coconut half and clambers inside, closing the two shells around itself to make a shelter.

## The Veined Octopus

Octopuses often hide inside things that lie on the seabed, but this is different. It is the first time an invertebrate* has been recorded lugging around an object, with a plan to use it later. This takes real brain power!

When the danger has passed, the octopus "tiptoes" off on its long arms, gripping both shells awkwardly on either side of its body. The shells will also come in handy for ambushing a passing meal—yum!

*Invertebrates are animals that don't have a backbone.

# Tools for Protection

Tools can be used for shelter and protection. These orangutans in Sumatra are adapting to their habitat by using objects to make themselves comfortable and keep themselves safe.

Rain pours down over the forest. This young **orangutan** is sheltering beneath a huge leaf that he holds like an umbrella. His mother has made herself a large leafy hat to keep her head dry.

In some parts of the island, orangutans use leaves as gloves. The leaves protect their hands from sharp prickles as they dig into spiky durian fruit. (Delicious but very smelly!)

The tasty seeds of the neesia fruit are surrounded by needlelike hairs, which could hurt the orangutans' mouths. In some areas, orangutans use a small stick to safely wiggle out the seeds to eat.

At the end of a long day, an ape needs a safe place to sleep. Orangutans roam for miles around the forest, and will build a new nest each evening up in the trees.

This resourceful female chooses strong, thick branches to make a sturdy cradle. She keeps these attached to the tree, only half breaking the branches so they can be woven together.

Next, she uses smaller, softer sticks to form a comfy mattress, and clumps of leafy twigs to make a pillow. She bites off sharp ends so she and her baby won't be poked in the night.

*Sometimes orangutans weave together more branches to make a waterproof roof, or a top bunk a few feet above the main nest.*

*Nest building isn't strictly tool use, but some researchers have called these complicated platforms "tools for sleeping!"*

*Orangutans in Sumatra blow good night "raspberries" as they climb into the nest!*

The orangutans cover themselves with a blanket of leafy branches, all ready for a good night's sleep.

In West Africa, a tap-tap-tapping echoes around the rain forest. A chimpanzee is cracking open a nut.

She places the nut on top of a flat rock that she grips with her feet. Then she pounds it with a stone—hard enough to break its shell but not so hard that she smashes the tasty nut inside.

# The Chimpanzees

These chimps, living in the Taï National Park in Côte d'Ivoire, have entered their own Stone Age. They are using tools somewhat like those used by our Stone Age human ancestors.

Primate archaeologists discovered that this area is full of stone tools that were used by chimps more than four thousand years ago!

There were lots of clues that these ancient tools hadn't belonged to humans. Some were covered in the residue of nuts that humans don't eat, and many of them were much heavier than stone tools used by people.

*It is unusual for primates to use stone tools. They tend to use tools made from plants—probably because they spend so much time in forests.*

## JUST LIKE YOU . . .

These young chimps are learning new skills, just as you learn by watching and practicing. It takes years of trial and error to get it right! The stones and rocks are like hammers and anvils.

# Are Tool-Users Smart?

Some tool-using creatures have big brains like these clever chimps, who are learning by trying out a new problem-solving idea . . .

The chimps have gathered to drink from a tree hollow, in Uganda's Budongo Forest. Usually they soak up hard-to-reach water with little sponges made from chewed leaves. But one of the chimps has had a new idea.

He has pulled some moss from the tree and is using it to absorb water from the hollow. He pops the spongy drinking tool into his mouth to quench his thirst. Some of the others try it too, and the idea spreads.

The chimps are learning and adapting to make the most of their environment. They are using tools in a flexible way and showing signs of planning ahead, which only the most intelligent creatures can do.

Other animals, like this common tailorbird, use tools in a fixed way that can't be changed or adapted . . .

The little bird is using spider silk to stitch together two leaves. She pierces tiny holes around the edges of the growing foliage with her needlelike beak. Then she pulls the silky thread through the holes, joining the leaves together to make a deep pouch for her nest—a perfectly camouflaged shelter.

It seems like a smart idea but stitching with spider silk and plant fibres is just the tailorbird's natural instinct. This species has evolved to make nests in this way—their brains aren't big and complex enough to try out new tricks.

In Australia's Shark Bay, a bottlenose dolphin
is foraging for food along the ocean floor.
She is wearing a sponge on the end of her snout.

Sharp rocks and prickly sea urchins can cause
scrapes and scratches, but the sea sponge protects
her smooth beak as she roots around for fish to eat.

*Young dolphins stay with their
mother for four or five years—
plenty of time to learn this new skill.*

These dolphins are protecting themselves, just like you do when you wear knee pads, wrist guards, or a bike helmet.

*Dolphins like to play with all kinds of things, as though they are toys. But when an object is used to do a particular job, it becomes a tool.*

## The Bottlenose Dolphin

The dolphins here in Shark Bay are the first tool-using dolphins to be discovered in the world. But not all of them have learned this resourceful trick. Sponging is passed down from mother to daughter, and very occasionally to son. Scientists have traced it back to a single female that lived almost two hundred years ago! They've nicknamed her "Sponging Eve."

# Creatures and their Cultures

Sometimes, creatures living in a particular place have their own unique way of using tools. They do things differently in different areas, somewhat like humans do . . .

Different tool-using techniques can spring up because resourceful animals adapt their tool-use to their habitats, by making the most of things that they find there.

**Capuchin monkeys** in dry parts of Brazil use stone tools to dig in the ground for plant roots and tubers.

But in damp, tropical habitats they don't bother with all that digging because there is plenty of other food to eat.

**Woodpecker finches** in hot and dry parts of the Galápagos Islands use cactus spines to forage for insects.

But those living in wet areas—where cacti don't grow—hardly ever use tools. They don't seem to use twigs either—no need when there's a feast to be found everywhere they look!

Sometimes, intelligent tool-users may pick up tricks from their parents or other members of their group. This could be an important way that ideas spread. Scientists have debates about how much of this "social learning" goes on.

**Orangutans** in some parts of Sumatra poke sticks into tree hollows to find honey—delicious! But those living farther to the east of the island don't seem to do this.

In Borneo, orangutans wipe their chins with leafy napkins after a juicy meal, but not so in Sumatra!

On a tropical island in the South Pacific, a crow is busy toolmaking. She smooths and sharpens a thin twig and shapes the end to form a hook.

It is perfect for fishing out a feast of insects and larvae from this dead tree trunk she has found.

## The New Caledonian Crow

All over New Caledonia, crows are using similar tools for foraging on the ground and pulling grubs from deadwood. They design differently shaped tools with hooks for different jobs.

New Caledonian crows often carry around a favorite tool that will come in handy later. They are planning ahead, just like humans do. By making tools that can be used again and again, these birds save time and energy and avoid waste.

You might sharpen your favorite pencil so it's nice and pointy for writing, then carry it in your backpack for when you need it.

*Some tools are used to irritate the prey until it bites down on the end of the twig and can be dragged out of its hiding place.*

*These crows sometimes carry their prey on the end of a tool like a marshmallow! Humans are the only other species known to do this.*

# A Toolmaking Masterclass

After humans, New Caledonian crows are probably the most talented toolmakers in the animal kingdom. They make tools instinctively and they learn by trial and error too. Making tools takes much more brain power than using a simple stick that they have found.

## Tool Gallery

These clever crows craft tools of different shapes and sizes to fish out food from all kinds of places. Narrow tools, wider tools, tools that taper to a tip . . .

There are hooked tools made from slim sticks and blades of grass.

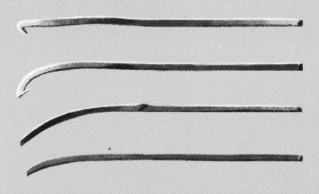

*These tools are made from stems, which have been carefully cut and bent to form a small hook.*

And there are tools torn from the leaves of the pandanus plant.

# How to Make a Pandanus Tool

The pandanus plant has lots of tiny hooklike spikes around the edges of its leaves, which make it handy as a tool.

1. The crow begins by cutting a long rectangle from the spiky leaf edge.

2. It carefully snips into the leaf with its beak.

3. It then tears downwards to make a step shape.

4. It snips then tears until it has a tool with a wide, sturdy end for holding, and a fine point for probing.

Fire crackles on grassland in Australia's Northern Territory.
A feeding frenzy breaks out as birds of prey dive onto grasshoppers,
lizards, and other small creatures that are scurrying from the blaze.

*Humans are believed to have been
using fire for more than a million
years, for cooking, warmth, light,
protection from predators, for making
tools, and to help with hunting.*

## The Fire-Foraging Raptors

Aboriginal peoples have known for thousands of years that
birds such as **black kites**, **whistling kites**, and **brown falcons**
sometimes use burning sticks as tools for spreading fire.

Waipuldanya Phillip Roberts OBE, who was an important
adviser on Aboriginal culture, recalled watching a raptor pick
up a smoldering stick in its claws and drop it in a fresh patch of
dry grass half a mile away.

These "firehawks" are using the flames to flush out prey as
they hunt. They are thought to be the only animals, apart
from humans, that have learned to use fire.

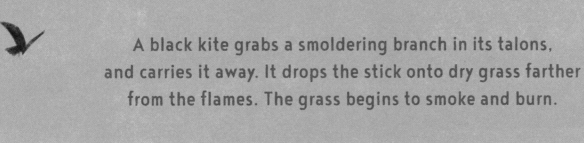

A black kite grabs a smoldering branch in its talons, and carries it away. It drops the stick onto dry grass farther from the flames. The grass begins to smoke and burn.

*A raptor is another name for a bird of prey—a bird that hunts animals such as mice, reptiles, and smaller birds.*

### JUST LIKE YOU . . .

These birds are transporting fire, just like an adult might use a match to light the candles on your birthday cake or a barbecue outside.

# Tools for Hunting and Trapping

Some creatures, including humans, use tools in grisly ways—as weapons for hunting, trapping, or defending.

### The Ants

Worker ants, in the Chihuahuan Desert of Mexico, wage war on rival ant colonies.

They pick up small stones with their powerful mandibles, and drop them into the entrance of the nest. They are sealing off their rival's homes so they can't eat all the food!

### The Chimpanzee

In Senegal, a chimpanzee brandishes a spear as she searches for prey. She's made this hunting tool by stripping the leaves from a long branch and sharpening it to a point.

## The Boxer Crab

A boxer crab in Hawaii is threatening another crab with a pair of stinging anemones. It carries the colorful sea creatures in its claws like pompoms, which it waggles aggressively at its rival. The two crabs are competing for food.

## The Egyptian Vulture

This Egyptian vulture is throwing stones at a clutch of ostrich eggs and hammering with a pebble to crack the shells. It wants to gobble up the goo inside.

## The Alligator

An alligator in Louisiana has balanced sticks on his snout as he lurks near a colony of egrets. He is using the twigs to tempt the birds towards his toothy jaws as they search for nest-building material. One of these birds will be his dinner. SNAP!

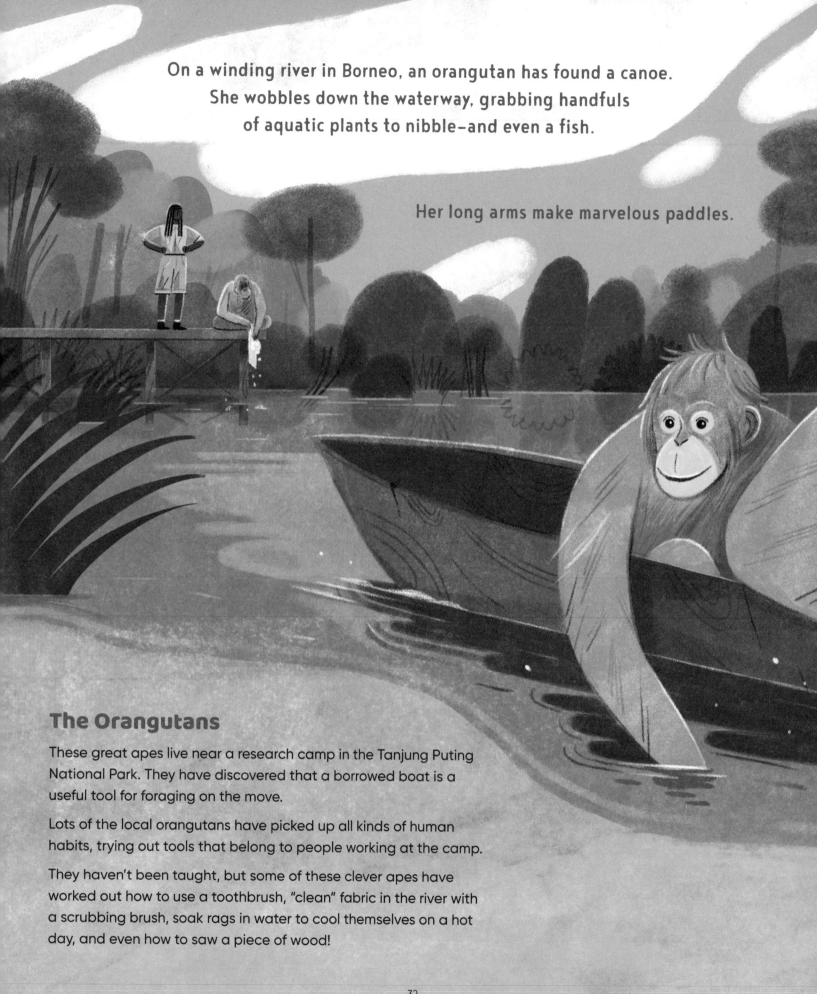

On a winding river in Borneo, an orangutan has found a canoe.
She wobbles down the waterway, grabbing handfuls
of aquatic plants to nibble—and even a fish.

Her long arms make marvelous paddles.

## The Orangutans

These great apes live near a research camp in the Tanjung Puting
National Park. They have discovered that a borrowed boat is a
useful tool for foraging on the move.

Lots of the local orangutans have picked up all kinds of human
habits, trying out tools that belong to people working at the camp.

They haven't been taught, but some of these clever apes have
worked out how to use a toothbrush, "clean" fabric in the river with
a scrubbing brush, soak rags in water to cool themselves on a hot
day, and even how to saw a piece of wood!

## JUST LIKE YOU . . .

This orangutan is using a boat, just like humans do, for fishing and traveling around. She seems to have learned by trying out new things, just as you often do.

*Orangutans like to take their time, watching carefully before jumping into a new task—probably one of the reasons they are good learners.*

# Curious Creatures and Curious Humans

Animals that live near humans adapt in all kinds of ways to survive and thrive. Resourceful tool-users find new ways of using objects to get things done. They may learn to avoid humans or stick around and make the most of human things . . .

## The Long-Tailed Macaques

This group of long-tailed macaques, living at a Buddhist temple in Thailand, use human hair to floss their teeth!

They pluck a few long strands from the heads of visitors to make a string, which they use to clear bits of food from between their gnashers.

The temple, in Lopburi, is famous for its macaques. They are treated with great respect and allowed to ride around on people's shoulders. The monkeys have adapted to spending so much time near hairy human heads!

Long-tailed macaques from the Nicobar Islands, in the Indian Ocean, floss with feathers or blades of grass instead.

## The Large-Billed Crows

In Tokyo, two large-billed crows are picking walnuts near a busy road. They drop the nuts onto the intersection below—right in front of cars waiting at the traffic lights.

The lights turn green, and the cars zoom forward, cracking open the nuts with their wheels. When it's safe, the crows hop along with the other pedestrians to collect their meal. They have learned to use the cars as powerful nutcrackers!

We humans have supercharged our lives with tools
and technology like no other creature on Earth.

But all around our busy planet, animals are working hard too.

When these amazing creatures toil with tools,
we catch a glimpse inside their minds and learn
about the things that connect us.

They remind us to work with our natural
environment, to be resourceful, and to reuse
the objects that help us every day.

Perhaps these curious creatures and their crafty ways
have more to teach us than we ever imagined.